# BEGINNERS GUIDE FOR SAMSUNG GALAXY S24 ULTRA

Navigating the Galaxy S24 Ultra Features, Tips, and
More  for a Seamless User Experience

**BRIAN Y. MARTIN**

# TABLE OF CONTENT

# INTRODUCTION

In a world where technology dances on the edge of innovation, the Samsung Galaxy S24 Ultra emerges as a beacon, a testament to the extraordinary possibilities that reside within the confines of a smartphone. As we delve into the intricacies of this technological marvel, be prepared for a journey that transcends the ordinary, unlocking a realm where design, performance, and features converge in perfect harmony.

Imagine cradling in your palm a device that is not just a phone but a piece of art. The Galaxy S24 Ultra's design transcends the mundane, a symphony of sleek elegance and ergonomic brilliance. It's not merely a device; it's an extension of your style, a tactile delight that fits seamlessly into your daily life.

But don't be fooled by its external beauty; beneath the surface lies a powerhouse. The Galaxy S24 Ultra is engineered for unparalleled performance. It navigates the complexities of modern life with ease, effortlessly transitioning between tasks, ensuring that you're always steps ahead. Efficiency, speed, and reliability are not just features – they're the essence of the S24 Ultra.

Now, let's talk about capturing life's moments in their purest form. The S24 Ultra's camera system is a visual storyteller, turning every click into a narrative. Whether you're a photography enthusiast or someone who cherishes the simplicity of a moment, this device transforms ordinary scenes into visual masterpieces. From breathtaking landscapes to intimate portraits, the S24 Ultra's camera system is a revelation.

As we continue this journey, brace yourself for features that redefine the boundaries of smartphone capabilities. The Galaxy S24 Ultra is not just a device; it's a technological odyssey, an invitation to explore new horizons. It's a companion that understands your needs, adapts to your lifestyle, and enhances every facet of your mobile experience.

In a world inundated with choices, the Samsung Galaxy S24 Ultra stands as a beacon of distinction, an embodiment of what happens when innovation and design converge seamlessly. Join us as we unravel the layers of this technological marvel and invite you to be a part of a future where the extraordinary is not just expected but delivered with every touch, click, and moment captured. The Galaxy S24 Ultra is not just a phone; it's an experience waiting to be explored.

# CHAPTER 1

# OVERVIEW AND KEY FEATURES

## Unveiling the Samsung Galaxy S24

In the ever-evolving landscape of smartphones, the Samsung Galaxy S24 stands as a formidable testament to technological advancement. This device is not just a phone; it's an embodiment of cutting-edge innovation that redefines our expectations of what a smartphone can be.

At first glance, the Galaxy S24 captivates with its sleek and elegant design. It's more than just a device; it's a statement of sophistication. The smooth curves and meticulously crafted details create an aesthetic appeal that goes beyond the ordinary. But this beauty is not just skin deep; it's an intentional design that seamlessly integrates into the user's lifestyle, offering not only visual pleasure but also ergonomic comfort.

What truly sets the Galaxy S24 apart is its display – a visual masterpiece that beckons users into a world of immersive experiences. The high-resolution screen delivers vibrant colors and sharp details, whether you're watching videos, playing games, or simply browsing. The display isn't just a canvas; it's a window to a world where every pixel contributes to a visual symphony that enhances the overall user experience.

Moving beyond aesthetics, the Galaxy S24's performance is a force to be reckoned with. Powered by state-of-the-art technology, this device ensures a seamless and efficient user experience. Apps launch instantly, multitasking is a breeze, and the overall responsiveness elevates the way we interact with our smartphones. The S24 is not just keeping up with the demands of modern life; it's setting new standards.

Now, let's delve into the heart of this technological marvel – the camera system. The Galaxy S24's camera isn't just a feature; it's a game-changer. Imagine capturing moments with unparalleled clarity and detail. From low-light scenes to high-action shots, the camera adapts to various environments, ensuring that every photo is a masterpiece. It's not just about taking pictures; it's about telling a visual story.

But the Galaxy S24 is not merely a collection of impressive specs; it's a device that understands and anticipates the user's needs. The user interface is intuitive, making navigation a breeze. The seamless integration of software and hardware enhances the overall user experience, creating a device that feels like an extension of oneself.

Connectivity is another realm where the Galaxy S24 shines. With 5G capabilities, the device ensures fast and reliable connections, opening up possibilities for seamless communication and content consumption. The S24 is not just a phone; it's a portal to a connected world where information flows effortlessly.

## The Evolution of Samsung's Galaxy Series

In tracing the evolution of Samsung's Galaxy series, we witness a remarkable journey through the annals of smartphone history. The Galaxy series isn't just a collection of devices; it's a testament to Samsung's commitment to pushing boundaries and shaping the future of mobile technology.

The inception of the Galaxy series marked a turning point in the industry, introducing smartphones that seamlessly blended style with functionality. From the early Galaxy models to the present, each iteration has been a step forward, a refinement of both design and performance.

As we navigate through the timeline, we encounter the Galaxy series' commitment to innovation. Features that were once considered revolutionary have become standard, as Samsung consistently raises the bar for what users can expect from their smartphones. From the introduction of Super AMOLED displays to advancements in camera technology, each Galaxy device has brought something new and groundbreaking to the table.

The design philosophy of the Galaxy series has also undergone a significant transformation. What began as a quest for sleekness and elegance has evolved into a holistic approach, considering not just aesthetics but also the feel and functionality of the device. The evolution is not just about making a phone look good; it's about creating a device that seamlessly integrates into the user's lifestyle.

Performance has always been a cornerstone of the Galaxy series. The progression from one model to the next is marked by leaps in processing power, memory capacity, and overall efficiency. The Galaxy series isn't just keeping pace with technological advancements; it's at the forefront, driving innovation and setting new standards for what a smartphone can achieve.

The Galaxy series is not a static entity; it's a living testament to Samsung's adaptability and responsiveness to user needs. With each new release, the company takes into account feedback, incorporating improvements and enhancements to create a user experience that is not just cutting-edge but also user-centric.

Connectivity has been a focal point in the evolution of the Galaxy series. As the world became more interconnected, Samsung responded by introducing features like enhanced network capabilities, creating devices that facilitate seamless communication and content consumption. The Galaxy series isn't just about individual devices; it's about being part of a connected ecosystem.

The evolution of Samsung's Galaxy series is a journey that reflects the dynamic nature of the smartphone industry. From its humble beginnings to the present, the Galaxy series stands as a testament to Samsung's unwavering dedication to innovation and user experience. As we look back at the series' evolution, we can anticipate that the future holds even more exciting developments, further solidifying Samsung's position as a trailblazer in the world of mobile technology.

## Screen Size

The Samsung Galaxy S24 Ultra's screen size is a visual marvel that transforms how we engage with content. With a generously large display, it offers an immersive viewing experience, making it perfect for anything from binge-watching your favorite shows to enhancing productivity. The bezel-less design ensures a seamless, edge-to-edge visual journey, eliminating distractions for a captivating experience. The high resolution delivers stunning clarity and vibrant colors, enriching the overall viewing pleasure. Navigating settings for the screen on the S24 Ultra is simple; explore the "Display" options in the Settings menu to customize brightness, enable adaptive display, and delve into various screen modes. The device's user-friendly interface enhances the overall experience, making it not just a phone but a visual delight tailored to your preferences.

## Battery and Charging Speed

The battery and charging speed of the Samsung Galaxy S24 Ultra are designed to keep up with your dynamic lifestyle. Featuring a high-capacity battery, it ensures long-lasting endurance, providing power throughout the day without the constant worry of running out. Smart battery management optimizes usage, intelligently managing processes to maximize battery life. Charging the S24 Ultra is not just routine; it's a fast-paced experience. The device supports fast charging technology, offering a quick boost to your battery levels. Wireless charging adds convenience to the mix, providing a cable-free and clutter-free charging experience. In the Settings menu, under "Battery," you can customize charging preferences, enabling fast charging and exploring advanced options. Efficient memory management plays a crucial role in optimizing battery performance, ensuring the S24 Ultra adapts to your needs, making power not a limitation but a facilitator.

## Memory

The memory capabilities of the Samsung Galaxy S24 Ultra redefine how we manage and access our digital world. Offering ample storage capacity, it ensures space for photos, videos, apps, and more. The device supports expandable memory through a microSD card slot, providing flexibility to accommodate your growing digital library. Efficient RAM management is at the core of seamless multitasking. With ample RAM, the S24 Ultra ensures smooth transitions between apps and tasks, enhancing the overall user experience. The Settings menu, particularly "Device care," provides insights into storage usage, allowing you to optimize storage and make the most of the available space. RAM-related options in the same menu offer customization for memory management, striking the perfect balance between performance and efficiency. The Samsung Galaxy S24 Ultra's memory capabilities go beyond capacity; they are enablers of a seamless and dynamic digital experience.

# CHAPTER 2

# DESIGN AND DISPLAY

## Sleek Aesthetics and Ergonomic Design

Exploring the marriage of sleek aesthetics and ergonomic design in smartphones unveils a captivating journey through form and function. It's not merely about creating visually appealing devices; it's about crafting a seamless user experience that begins the moment the device is held.

The pursuit of sleek aesthetics isn't just about making a phone look good; it's an art form. From the curvature of the edges to the placement of buttons, every detail is carefully considered. The goal is to create a device that not only catches the eye but also feels like an extension of the user's style. The sleekness isn't just superficial; it's a deliberate choice to enhance the overall user experience.

But aesthetics alone do not define the essence of a smartphone. The integration of ergonomic design takes the user experience to a whole new level. It's about more than just holding a device; it's about how the device fits into the contours of the user's hand. The placement of buttons, the weight distribution, and the overall feel are meticulously crafted to ensure comfort during prolonged use.

The synergy between sleek aesthetics and ergonomic design is evident in every curve and contour of the device. The device becomes an object of desire, not just for its visual appeal but for the tactile satisfaction it provides. It's a marriage of style and substance, creating a symbiotic relationship between the visual allure and the practical usability of the device.

As we explore this intricate dance between form and function, it becomes clear that the combination of sleek aesthetics and ergonomic design isn't a mere luxury; it's a necessity. It's about creating devices that not only stand out in a crowded market but also offer a user experience that goes beyond expectations.

In the world of smartphones, the marriage of sleek aesthetics and ergonomic design isn't just a design philosophy; it's a commitment to creating devices that delight the senses and seamlessly integrate into the user's lifestyle. It's about more than just holding a device; it's about forging a connection between the user and the technology they hold in their hands.

## Immersive Visual Experience on the S24 Display

Dive into the immersive realm of the Samsung Galaxy S24 Ultra's display, where every pixel becomes a portal to an extraordinary visual experience. It's not just a screen; it's a canvas that transcends the boundaries of conventional displays, inviting users into a world of unparalleled clarity, vibrancy, and engagement.

The S24 Ultra's display is a symphony of technological brilliance. The high resolution ensures that every image, video, or text is rendered with exquisite detail. Whether you're watching a cinematic masterpiece or scrolling through your favorite social media feed, the clarity of the display elevates the visual experience to new heights.

But it's not just about the sharpness of the visuals; it's about the colors that come to life on the screen. The S24 Ultra's display boasts vibrant and true-to-life colors that make every image pop. Whether it's the rich hues of a sunset or the subtle tones of a black-and-white photograph, the display reproduces colors with remarkable accuracy, creating a visual feast for the eyes.

The immersive experience extends beyond just static images. The S24 Ultra's display is designed to handle dynamic content with finesse. From smooth transitions in videos to seamless gameplay, the display's responsiveness ensures that every interaction is fluid and lag-free. It's not just about what you see; it's about how you experience it.

The bezel-less design of the S24 Ultra's display enhances the immersive factor. With minimal distractions, users are drawn into the content, whether it's a captivating movie or an intense gaming session. The edge-to-edge display maximizes the screen real estate, making every inch a canvas for creativity and engagement.

As we delve into the immersive visual experience on the S24 Ultra's display, it becomes clear that it's not just a feature; it's a cornerstone of the device's identity. It's about more than just viewing content; it's about being transported into the heart of the action, whether it's a virtual world, a stunning photograph, or a compelling video.

In a world where visuals play a pivotal role in our digital interactions, the Samsung Galaxy S24 Ultra's display is not just a window to content; it's a gateway to a visual journey that captivates, inspires, and leaves an indelible impression. It's not just about seeing; it's about experiencing, and the S24 Ultra's display ensures that every visual encounter is nothing short of extraordinary.

# CHAPTER 3

## POWER AND PERFORMANCE

### Unleashing the Potential Performance Features

The S24 Ultra's performance features are more than just specifications; they are the driving force behind an efficient and responsive user experience. Imagine a device that launches apps in the blink of an eye, effortlessly juggles multiple tasks, and navigates through the complexities of modern life with unparalleled ease. This isn't just about speed; it's about a performance that adapts to your pace.

At the heart of this technological powerhouse lies a processor that doesn't just meet expectations; it exceeds them. The S24 Ultra is engineered to handle the demands of today's dynamic digital landscape. Whether you're streaming high-definition content, engaging in graphics-intensive gaming, or running resource-intensive applications, the device responds with a level of performance that is nothing short of exceptional.

But performance isn't just about brute force; it's about optimization and efficiency. The S24 Ultra intelligently manages resources, ensuring that every component works in harmony to deliver a smooth and lag-free experience. It's not just a phone; it's a well-orchestrated symphony of technology that anticipates your needs and delivers a performance that feels tailor-made.

Multitasking is not a challenge for the S24 Ultra; it's a core strength. Picture seamlessly switching between applications, effortlessly moving from work to entertainment, all without missing a beat. The device's prowess in multitasking isn't just a convenience; it's a testament to a performance that aligns with the dynamic nature of our daily lives.

The S24 Ultra's performance features extend beyond just the hardware; they encompass the entire user interface. Navigating through the device is an intuitive experience, with smooth transitions and responsive interactions. It's not just about what the device can do;

it's about how effortlessly it becomes an extension of your intentions.

As we delve into the unleashed potential of the S24 Ultra's performance features, it's evident that this device is not just keeping pace with technological advancements; it's defining them. It's a declaration that performance is not a compromise but a standard, setting a new benchmark for what users can expect from their smartphones.

In a world where efficiency and speed are paramount, the Samsung Galaxy S24 Ultra's performance features aren't just a feature list; they are the heartbeat of a device that empowers users to navigate through the digital landscape with confidence and unmatched capability. It's not just about what you can do; it's about what the S24 Ultra enables you to achieve.

## Navigating Multitasking with Ease

It's a seamless and intuitive experience, courtesy of the Samsung Galaxy S24 Ultra. The device doesn't just accommodate multitasking; it embraces it, offering a user experience that effortlessly navigates through the demands of a dynamic and interconnected digital lifestyle.

Imagine a scenario where you can effortlessly switch between applications, respond to messages while streaming your favorite music, and seamlessly transition from work to play without missing a beat. This is the reality of multitasking on the S24 Ultra – a reality where the device adapts to your needs, allowing you to navigate through different facets of your life with unparalleled ease.

The S24 Ultra's approach to multitasking is more than just split-screen functionalities; it's about creating an environment where every interaction feels natural and fluid. Picture replying to emails while referring to documents, taking notes during a video call, or even watching a tutorial while experimenting with a new app – all in a manner that is as intuitive as it is efficient.

The device's hardware and software work in tandem to ensure that multitasking is not a cumbersome process but an integral part of your daily workflow. The processor's power, coupled with the intelligent resource management, allows you to run multiple applications simultaneously without compromising performance. It's not just about doing more; it's about doing more without the hassle.

Switching between applications on the S24 Ultra is a breeze, thanks to an interface that understands the nuances of multitasking. The transitions are smooth, and the learning curve is minimal, making it accessible to users of all levels of technical expertise. It's not just about the features; it's about how effortlessly you can integrate them into your daily routine.

Whether you're a professional juggling work-related tasks, a student managing research and assignments, or simply someone who likes to stay connected to various aspects of life simultaneously, the S24 Ultra's approach to multitasking ensures that the device is not a hindrance but a facilitator. It's about empowering users to navigate through the complexities of modern life without feeling overwhelmed.

As we explore the realm of navigating multitasking with ease on the Samsung Galaxy S24 Ultra, it becomes clear that this device isn't just a tool; it's a companion that understands the fluid nature of our daily lives. It's not just about having multiple apps open; it's about having the freedom to seamlessly transition between them, allowing you to make the most of every moment without compromise. Welcome to a world where multitasking is not a challenge; it's a delightful experience.

## Processor, RAM Management, Gaming

The Samsung Galaxy S24 Ultra stands as a pinnacle of technological achievement, seamlessly integrating a powerful processor, efficient RAM management, and a gaming experience that sets a new standard for mobile devices.

At the heart of the Galaxy S24 Ultra's capabilities is its advanced processor. Engineered to meet the demands of contemporary users, this processor serves as the powerhouse that drives the device's seamless operations. Whether you're launching applications, multitasking, or engaging in resource-intensive tasks, the processor ensures swift and responsive performance.

This advanced processor isn't solely about raw speed. It embodies a strategic blend of power and efficiency, leveraging cutting-edge technology to strike a balance between high-performance capabilities and optimal power consumption. This equilibrium ensures that while the device delivers exceptional speed and responsiveness, it also prioritizes energy efficiency, contributing to an extended battery life.

Efficient RAM management complements the processor's capabilities, providing a seamless multitasking experience. The Galaxy S24 Ultra boasts ample RAM, allowing it to effortlessly handle multiple applications running simultaneously. This ensures smooth transitions between tasks without any noticeable lag, offering users a consistently high level of performance.

The intelligent RAM management system goes beyond the basic allocation of resources. It optimizes the utilization of the available RAM, adapting to user behavior and preferences. This results in a device that not only performs well during everyday tasks but also maintains its efficiency during demanding usage scenarios.

Gaming on the Galaxy S24 Ultra is a thrilling experience, courtesy of the combination of a powerful processor, efficient RAM management, and advanced graphics capabilities. Whether you're a casual gamer or a dedicated enthusiast, the device caters to your gaming needs with high frame rates, smooth gameplay, and immersive graphics.

The device's gaming prowess is not limited to specific genres or titles; it extends across the gaming spectrum. Graphics-intensive games come to life with vivid details, and even casual gaming sessions benefit from the device's ability to deliver a lag-free and enjoyable experience. The Galaxy S24 Ultra is not just a communication tool but also a portable gaming console that ensures every gaming moment is captivating.

Exploring the processor and performance settings on the Galaxy S24 Ultra is a user-friendly experience. The device provides customization options to cater to individual preferences and usage patterns. In the Settings menu, under categories like "Performance" or similar, users can find options to optimize performance based on their specific needs. This level of customization ensures that users can tailor the device's performance to suit their preferences, even if they're not tech-savvy.

Beyond the gaming realm, the processor and performance capabilities of the Galaxy S24 Ultra extend to everyday tasks and resource-intensive activities. Streaming high-definition content, editing photos and videos, or engaging in other demanding applications – the device consistently delivers a smooth and responsive performance.

The processor's efficiency is particularly evident in power management. The Galaxy S24 Ultra intelligently allocates resources, optimizing energy usage for sustained performance. This ensures that the device isn't just about speed but also about intelligent resource allocation, contributing to an overall efficient and satisfying user experience.

# CHAPTER 4

## CAMERA EXCELLENCE

### S24 Ultra's Advanced Camera System

**E**mbark on a visual odyssey as we delve into the advanced camera system of the Samsung Galaxy S24 Ultra, a technological marvel that goes beyond capturing moments; it redefines the art of photography. This isn't just about megapixels and lenses; it's a journey into the intricate details of settings, capabilities, and features that make the S24 Ultra's camera system a true pioneer in the realm of smartphone photography.

At the core of the S24 Ultra's camera system is a sensor that captures not just images but stories. With a high megapixel count, the device ensures that every detail is preserved with stunning clarity. From the subtleties of texture to the brilliance of color, the camera invites users to explore a world of visual richness.

But the S24 Ultra's camera isn't just about quantity; it's about quality. The sensor is optimized to perform exceptionally well in various lighting conditions. Whether it's a sun-drenched landscape or a dimly lit indoor scene, the device adapts, ensuring that your photos are a true reflection of the moment, devoid of overexposure or loss of detail.

One of the standout features of the S24 Ultra's camera system is its versatility. The device doesn't just boast a single lens; it embraces a multi-lens setup that caters to different photography scenarios. From wide-angle shots that capture expansive landscapes to telephoto lenses that bring distant subjects closer, the S24 Ultra ensures that you have the right tool for every photographic endeavor.

Settings play a crucial role in shaping the outcome of your photos, and the S24 Ultra empowers users with an array of options. Manual mode allows for a hands-on approach, giving enthusiasts the ability to tweak settings such as shutter speed, ISO, and white balance. It's not just about taking a photo; it's about crafting an image with precision and intention.

The S24 Ultra's camera system doesn't just stop at photography; it's a force to be reckoned with in the realm of videography. The device supports high-resolution video recording with advanced stabilization features, ensuring that your videos are not just moments captured in motion but cinematic experiences.

Artificial intelligence is woven into the fabric of the S24 Ultra's camera capabilities. From scene recognition that optimizes settings based on what you're capturing to smart features that enhance facial expressions and detect smiles, the device becomes an intuitive photography companion. It's not just about point-and-shoot; it's about a camera system that understands the nuances of composition and expression.

Low-light photography is a realm where the S24 Ultra truly shines. The device leverages advanced algorithms and sensor capabilities to capture stunning details even in challenging lighting conditions. Night mode goes beyond just brightening the scene; it adds depth and clarity, transforming nighttime shots into visually arresting compositions.

The user interface of the camera app is designed with simplicity and functionality in mind. Navigating through modes, adjusting settings, and accessing features are intuitive processes, making the camera system accessible to users of all levels of expertise. It's not just about catering to photography enthusiasts; it's about ensuring that every user can harness the full potential of the camera system.

## Rear and front camera setup

The rear camera system is a powerhouse, bringing together multiple lenses to capture a wide range of perspectives. It's not just about megapixels; it's about a comprehensive approach to imaging that ensures every shot is a masterpiece.

At the heart of the rear camera system is its versatility. With a combination of wide-angle, ultra-wide, and telephoto lenses, the S24 Ultra covers the entire spectrum of focal lengths. This allows you to capture expansive landscapes, zoom in on distant subjects, and everything in between. The multi-lens setup is a testament to the device's commitment to providing users with a diverse and flexible photography toolkit.

The S24 Ultra's rear camera system isn't just about hardware; it integrates advanced software features to enhance your shooting experience. From intelligent scene recognition that optimizes settings based on what you're capturing to AI-powered enhancements that refine details and colors, the device ensures that your photos are not just images but visual stories.

Low-light photography is where the S24 Ultra truly shines. The device leverages advanced sensor technology and computational photography to capture stunning details even in challenging lighting conditions. Night mode takes low-light photography to the next level, ensuring that your nighttime shots are as vivid and detailed as those taken during the day.

The front camera of the S24 Ultra is no slouch either. Designed to capture stunning selfies, it goes beyond mere megapixels. With features like portrait mode and beauty enhancements, the front camera ensures that your self-portraits are Instagram-worthy. The device embraces the trend of high-quality video calls, providing crisp and clear video quality for virtual meetings or catching up with friends and family.

The front and rear cameras of the S24 Ultra work in harmony, ensuring a consistent and high-quality imaging experience across both setups. Whether you're capturing a scenic landscape with the rear camera or snapping a selfie with the front camera, the device maintains a cohesive and impressive imaging standard.

Exploring the camera settings on the S24 Ultra is a straightforward process. The camera interface is intuitive, allowing you to easily switch between different modes, adjust settings, and explore creative features. The Pro mode empowers photography enthusiasts to fine-tune settings like ISO, shutter speed, and white balance, providing a level of control typically found in professional cameras.

Video recording capabilities on the S24 Ultra are equally impressive. The device supports high-resolution video recording, with features like stabilization ensuring smooth footage even in dynamic situations. From capturing memorable family moments to shooting vlogs on the go, the S24 Ultra's camera system is a versatile tool for both photography and videography enthusiasts.

## Photography and Videography Tips

Elevate your photography and videography skills with the Samsung Galaxy S24 Ultra's advanced camera system. Whether you're a seasoned enthusiast or just getting started, these tips will help you make the most of the device's capabilities and unlock a new level of creative potential.

### 1. Understand Your Camera Modes

Familiarize yourself with the various camera modes available on the S24 Ultra. From Pro mode for manual adjustments to Night mode for low-light situations, each mode is designed to cater to specific scenarios. Experimenting with these modes allows you to capture diverse and stunning shots.

## 2. Optimize Settings in Pro Mode

If you enjoy having more control over your shots, explore Pro mode. Adjust settings like ISO, shutter speed, and white balance to fine-tune your photos. Pro mode is a powerful tool for achieving the desired look and feel in different lighting conditions.

## 3. Master Composition Techniques

Enhance the visual appeal of your photos by applying basic composition techniques. Experiment with the rule of thirds, leading lines, and framing to create captivating and well-balanced shots. These techniques can turn an ordinary scene into a visually striking composition.

## 4. Utilize Smart Features

Leverage the intelligent features of the S24 Ultra's camera, such as scene recognition and AI enhancements. These features automatically optimize settings based on the subject, ensuring that your photos look their best without manual adjustments.

## 5. Explore Different Lenses

Take advantage of the multiple lenses on the S24 Ultra. Switch between wide-angle, standard, and telephoto lenses to capture a variety of perspectives. Each lens offers a unique way to frame your subjects, adding versatility to your photography.

## 6. Experiment with Night Mode

Night mode on the S24 Ultra is a game-changer for low-light photography. When shooting in challenging lighting conditions, switch to Night mode to capture detailed and well-exposed photos. Keep the device steady for a few seconds to allow the camera to work its magic.

## 7. Capture Cinematic Videos

When shooting videos, explore the device's video capabilities. Experiment with different frame rates and resolutions to achieve the desired cinematic look. The S24 Ultra's stabilization features ensure smooth footage, even in dynamic or fast-paced scenes.

## 8. Use AI for Dynamic Shots

Take advantage of AI features for dynamic shots. The AI can recognize and track subjects, making it easier to capture moving objects or people. This is especially useful for action shots or when you want to focus on a specific element in the frame.

### 9. Edit with Precision

After capturing your shots, explore the editing tools within the camera app. Adjust exposure, contrast, and color to refine your images. The S24 Ultra's editing features allow you to enhance your photos directly on the device without the need for external applications.

### 10. Experiment and Have Fun

The most important tip is to experiment and have fun with your photography and videography. The S24 Ultra's camera system offers a wealth of features and creative tools. Don't be afraid to try new things, explore different settings, and let your creativity flow.

By incorporating these tips into your photography and videography endeavors, you'll be able to maximize the potential of the Samsung Galaxy S24 Ultra's advanced camera system and capture moments in a way that reflects your unique style and vision. Happy shooting!

# CHAPTER 5

## INNOVATIVE FEATURES

### Exploring the Cutting-Edge Features of the S24

At first glance, the S24 Ultra captivates with its sleek and ergonomic design. It's not just a device; it's a visual masterpiece meticulously crafted for both style and comfort. The slim profile and ergonomic curves make it a delight to hold, setting the stage for an elevated user experience.

Moving beyond aesthetics, the S24 Ultra's display is a visual marvel. It's not just a screen; it's a vibrant canvas that brings content to life with stunning clarity and vibrant colors. Whether you're immersed in videos, engaged in gaming, or simply browsing, the display provides an unparalleled visual experience.

Underpinning the S24 Ultra's prowess is its advanced camera system. Beyond megapixels, this system is a storyteller that captures moments with precision and artistry. From versatile lenses that adapt to different scenarios to AI features that enhance your photography, the S24 Ultra empowers users to unleash their creativity.

Performance is where the S24 Ultra truly shines. Powered by cutting-edge technology, the device ensures seamless multitasking and responsiveness. It's not just about keeping up with tasks; it's about setting the pace, providing a level of efficiency that aligns with the dynamic demands of modern life.

Connectivity is another frontier where the S24 Ultra excels. With 5G capabilities, the device ensures fast and reliable connections, opening up possibilities for seamless communication and content consumption. The S24 Ultra isn't just a phone; it's a portal to a connected world where information flows effortlessly.

Venturing into the software realm, the S24 Ultra's user interface is designed for intuitive navigation. It's not just about features; it's about how effortlessly users can interact with the device. The interface adapts to user needs, creating an experience that feels natural and user-friendly.

Exploring the device's features takes us into the realm of customization. The S24 Ultra allows users to tailor their experience with personalized settings, themes, and configurations. It's not just a device; it's a reflection of individual preferences, ensuring that each user's journey is unique.

Security is a paramount concern, and the S24 Ultra addresses this with cutting-edge biometric features. From fingerprint recognition to facial authentication, the device provides multiple layers of security, ensuring that user data remains protected.

Battery life is a crucial aspect of any smartphone, and the S24 Ultra doesn't disappoint. With advanced battery optimization features, the device ensures longevity, allowing users to stay connected throughout the day without the constant worry of running out of power.

## Unique Functions that Set the S24 Apart

This device transcends the ordinary, introducing functionalities that go beyond standard features, making it a standout in the ever-evolving realm of mobile technology.

The S24 Ultra's design is a marvel of innovation, seamlessly blending aesthetics with functionality. It goes beyond visual appeal, offering a slim profile and ergonomic curves that make it a unique piece of technological art. Holding the S24 Ultra is not just holding a phone; it's cradling a symbol of design ingenuity.

The multi-lens camera system is a revolutionary aspect that sets the S24 Ultra apart. It's not just about megapixels; it's a photographic powerhouse that redefines smartphone photography. Wide-angle shots, telephoto lenses – the S24 Ultra's camera system offers versatility that opens up new possibilities for capturing moments.

Artificial intelligence (AI) takes center stage in personalizing the user experience. The S24 Ultra adapts and learns user preferences, anticipating needs and tailoring settings accordingly. Whether it's suggesting optimal camera settings or managing battery life based on daily routines, the S24 Ultra becomes a personalized companion.

Performance optimization reaches new heights with the S24 Ultra. It's not just about raw power; it's about dynamic adaptability. The device intelligently allocates resources based on usage patterns, ensuring that performance is not only powerful but also efficiently managed. It's a unique blend of strength and smart resource utilization.

The edge-to-edge display is not just a visual treat; it's an immersive experience. Maximizing screen real estate, the S24 Ultra eliminates distractions with its bezel-less design, providing users with an unbroken visual canvas for their digital interactions.

Multitasking on the S24 Ultra is not just a feature; it's an expertise. The device seamlessly handles multiple applications, allowing users to switch between tasks effortlessly. It's about creating an environment where multitasking feels natural, whether you're responding to messages while watching a video or juggling work-related tasks.

Cutting-edge connectivity is a hallmark of the S24 Ultra. Embracing 5G, the device provides fast and reliable connections, keeping users seamlessly connected to the world around them. It's not just about faster internet; it's about meeting the demands of constant connectivity in the modern world.

Navigating the S24 Ultra's interface is a uniquely intuitive experience. It's not just about features; it's about how effortlessly users can interact with the device. The interface adapts to user habits, creating an environment where every touch, swipe, and interaction feels intuitive and user-friendly.

Security takes a front seat with the S24 Ultra's biometric innovations. From fingerprint recognition to facial authentication, the device employs multiple layers of security. It's not just about unlocking the phone; it's about ensuring that user data remains protected with cutting-edge biometric technologies.

Customization options abound with the S24 Ultra, going beyond boundaries to embrace individuality. It's not just a device; it's a canvas for users to express their unique preferences. From customizable themes to personalized settings, the device ensures that each user can tailor their experience, making it truly their own.

The Samsung Galaxy S24 Ultra is not just another smartphone; it's a culmination of unique functions that elevate it to a league of its own. From design innovation to revolutionary camera capabilities, from AI-powered personalization to cutting-edge connectivity, the S24 Ultra sets new standards for what a smartphone can offer. It's not just a device; it's an embodiment of innovation and distinction in the world of mobile technology. Welcome to a realm where uniqueness isn't just a feature; it's the very essence of the Samsung Galaxy S24 Ultra.

# CHAPTER 6

## CONNECTIVITY AND NETWORK

### Seamless Connectivity 5G and Beyond

**B**eyond the conventional features, the S24 Ultra's connectivity is a testament to innovation, setting new standards and redefining what users can expect from a smartphone in the realm of connectivity.

At the core of the S24 Ultra's connectivity prowess is its embrace of 5G technology. It's not just about faster internet; it's about entering a new era of connectivity where speed, reliability, and low latency converge to create an unparalleled user experience. The device ensures that users are at the forefront of this revolution, with 5G capabilities opening up possibilities that were once beyond reach.

Streaming high-definition content, engaging in video calls with crystal-clear quality, and downloading large files in the blink of an eye – the S24 Ultra's 5G connectivity makes these tasks not just efficient but seamless. It's about more than just speed; it's about a transformative shift in how we interact with the digital world, unburdened by lag or interruptions.

But the S24 Ultra doesn't stop at 5G; it goes beyond to explore the future of connectivity. As technology evolves, the device ensures that users are equipped to navigate the ever-expanding landscape of connected possibilities. The S24 Ultra becomes not just a phone but a gateway to a world where connectivity is not a limitation but an enabler.

Beyond the technicalities, the S24 Ultra's connectivity is about staying seamlessly connected to the people, content, and information that matter. It's not just a device; it's a portal to a connected ecosystem where communication knows no bounds. Whether it's staying in touch with loved ones, collaborating on work projects, or indulging in digital entertainment, the S24 Ultra ensures that users are always a step ahead.

The device's intelligent connectivity management ensures that it optimizes resources for a seamless experience. It's not just about having a fast connection; it's about having a smart connection that adapts to user needs. The S24 Ultra intelligently juggles multiple tasks, ensuring that connectivity is a facilitator rather than a barrier.

The S24 Ultra's commitment to seamless connectivity extends beyond the traditional realms. With the rise of the Internet of Things (IoT), the device becomes a hub for a connected lifestyle. Whether it's controlling smart home devices, tracking fitness metrics through wearables, or accessing information across interconnected devices, the S24 Ultra is a central player in the connected ecosystem.

Security is a paramount concern in the interconnected world, and the S24 Ultra addresses this with advanced security features. From secure data transmission over 5G networks to biometric authentication, the device ensures that users can enjoy the benefits of connectivity without compromising on privacy and security.

Navigating the S24 Ultra's connectivity is a user-friendly experience. It's not just about the technicalities of network protocols; it's about how effortlessly users can leverage the connectivity features. The device's interface simplifies the process, ensuring that even those less tech-savvy can harness the power of seamless connectivity.

The Samsung Galaxy S24 Ultra's connectivity is a journey into the future of connected experiences. It's not just about 5G; it's about embracing a world where connectivity is fast, reliable, and intelligent. The S24 Ultra becomes a companion in the connected era, where staying in touch, accessing information, and navigating a world of possibilities is not just a task but a seamless and integral part of everyday life. Welcome to a future where connectivity isn't just a feature; it's a transformative force, and the Samsung Galaxy S24 Ultra leads the way.

## Enhancing User Experience through Connectivity

Beyond the traditional notions of staying connected, the S24 Ultra redefines the role of connectivity, seamlessly weaving it into the fabric of the user experience and elevating the way we interact with the digital world.

At the heart of the S24 Ultra's connectivity prowess is its commitment to providing users with an experience that goes beyond the ordinary. It's not just about being connected; it's about being connected in a way that enhances every facet of the user's digital life.

The device's embrace of 5G technology stands as a cornerstone of this enhanced connectivity experience. It's not merely about faster internet speeds; it's about entering a realm where the digital and physical worlds converge seamlessly. With 5G capabilities, the S24 Ultra opens up avenues for high-speed streaming, low-latency gaming, and instantaneous downloads – all contributing to a user experience that is not just efficient but revolutionary.

But the S24 Ultra's connectivity journey doesn't stop at 5G; it extends into the realm of anticipatory connectivity. The device becomes a companion that understands user habits and preferences, optimizing connectivity to align with individual needs. Whether it's pre-loading content for a seamless streaming experience or anticipating data requirements for efficient multitasking, the S24 Ultra ensures that connectivity is not just a passive feature but an active facilitator.

The enhanced connectivity on the S24 Ultra is not just about speed; it's about reliability. The device intelligently manages network resources, ensuring a stable and consistent connection. Whether you're in a crowded urban area or a remote location, the S24 Ultra's connectivity adapts to deliver a reliable experience, eliminating the frustrations of dropped connections or lag.

The seamless connectivity experience extends beyond the traditional realms of internet browsing and calls. The S24 Ultra becomes a hub for an interconnected lifestyle. With the rise of the Internet of Things (IoT), the device seamlessly integrates with smart home devices, wearables, and other connected gadgets, offering users a central point for managing their connected ecosystem.

Security is a paramount consideration in the enhanced connectivity journey of the S24 Ultra. The device leverages advanced encryption protocols for secure data transmission over 5G networks. Biometric authentication adds an additional layer of security, ensuring that user data remains protected in the interconnected digital landscape.

The user interface of the S24 Ultra is designed with connectivity in mind. It's not just about technical intricacies; it's about how effortlessly users can navigate and leverage connectivity features. The interface is intuitive, ensuring that even those less familiar with the nuances of connectivity can seamlessly integrate it into their daily interactions.

# CHAPTER 7

# USER INTERFACE AND SOFTWARE

## Navigating the Galaxy Interface

The interface of the S24 Ultra is more than a collection of icons and menus; it's a gateway to a digital realm where every touch, swipe, and interaction feels intuitive. Navigating through the device becomes an effortlessly smooth experience, setting the stage for a user interface that adapts to individual preferences.

At the core of the S24 Ultra's interface design is simplicity without sacrificing functionality. It's not just about the number of features; it's about how those features are presented and accessed. The device ensures that users can effortlessly find what they need, streamlining the user experience and eliminating unnecessary complexities.

Customization takes center stage in the S24 Ultra's interface. It's not just about a one-size-fits-all approach; it's about tailoring the device to individual preferences. From customizable themes to personalized settings, the interface allows users to make the S24 Ultra truly their own, creating a digital environment that resonates with their unique style.

The interface seamlessly integrates AI-driven features that adapt to user habits. It's not just about static menus; it's about a dynamic experience that evolves with the user. The S24 Ultra learns preferences, anticipates needs, and offers smart suggestions, creating an interface that feels like a personalized assistant rather than a static platform.

Navigation through the S24 Ultra's interface is not confined to a single mode. It's about versatility, offering multiple ways for users to interact with the device. Whether it's gestures, voice commands, or traditional taps, the interface accommodates various input methods, ensuring that users can choose the method that suits them best.

The S24 Ultra's interface extends beyond the boundaries of the device itself. It becomes a gateway to a connected ecosystem. With seamless integration across devices and services, users can transition from the phone to other connected gadgets without disruption. It's not just about the phone; it's about a cohesive digital experience that extends across the user's tech landscape.

Security is seamlessly woven into the fabric of the S24 Ultra's interface. Biometric authentication methods, from fingerprint recognition to facial scanning, provide secure access to the device. It's not just about unlocking the phone; it's about ensuring that user data remains protected in an interconnected digital environment.

In conclusion, navigating the Galaxy interface of the Samsung Galaxy S24 Ultra is not just about moving through screens; it's about embarking on a user-centric journey. The device's interface is designed to simplify, personalize, and seamlessly integrate into the user's digital life. As we navigate through the S24 Ultra's interface, it becomes clear that this is more than just a means to access features; it's a dynamic and intuitive companion that enhances every touchpoint of the user's digital experience. Welcome to a world where navigating your device is not just a task; it's a delight, and the Samsung Galaxy S24 Ultra leads the way.

## Software Updates and Enhancements

The Samsung Galaxy S24 Ultra's commitment to staying at the forefront of technology is evident in its approach to software updates and enhancements. This isn't just a smartphone; it's a dynamic device that evolves with time, ensuring users have access to the latest features, security patches, and improvements.

Software updates play a crucial role in maintaining the Galaxy S24 Ultra's peak performance and security. Samsung regularly releases updates to the device's operating system, addressing any potential vulnerabilities, enhancing system stability, and introducing new features. These updates aren't just about fixing bugs; they are a proactive measure to ensure the device continues to deliver a seamless and secure user experience.

The software update process on the Galaxy S24 Ultra is user-friendly, reflecting Samsung's commitment to making technology accessible to all users. Notifications alert users when updates are available, and the device provides options for automatic updates, ensuring that users can effortlessly keep their device up to date. The Settings menu contains a dedicated section for software updates, allowing users to manually check for updates and initiate the installation process.

Beyond security and stability, software updates on the Galaxy S24 Ultra introduce exciting enhancements and features. Samsung listens to user feedback and adapts the device's software to meet evolving needs. Whether it's improvements in camera capabilities, refinements to the user interface, or the introduction of innovative features, software updates are a testament to Samsung's dedication to delivering an ever-improving user experience.

The Galaxy S24 Ultra's software updates are not limited to the core operating system; they extend to individual applications and services. Samsung's ecosystem receives regular updates, ensuring that apps like the camera, gallery, and productivity tools stay at the cutting edge of functionality. This ensures that users not only benefit from improvements in system-level performance but also from enhanced capabilities in their favorite applications.

Security is a top priority for Samsung, and this is evident in how the Galaxy S24 Ultra handles security updates. The device receives timely security patches that address potential vulnerabilities, providing users with peace of mind in an ever-evolving digital landscape. Samsung's commitment to regular security updates reflects a proactive approach to safeguarding user data and privacy.

The software enhancement journey on the Galaxy S24 Ultra goes beyond routine updates. Samsung embraces innovation, introducing major software upgrades that redefine the user experience. These upgrades may include entirely new versions of the operating system, delivering a fresh look, improved functionalities, and compatibility with the latest technologies. This commitment to major software upgrades ensures that the Galaxy S24 Ultra remains relevant and competitive in the fast-paced world of technology.

Samsung's user-friendly approach to software updates extends to the user interface. Navigating through the settings related to updates is intuitive, allowing users to customize update preferences and ensure a seamless update experience. The device's interface provides transparency, offering detailed information about the changes and improvements brought by each update.

The Samsung Galaxy S24 Ultra's approach to software updates and enhancements is a testament to the device's commitment to delivering a user experience that stands the test of time. It's not just about fixing bugs or addressing security concerns; it's about continuously improving and adapting to the evolving needs of users. The Galaxy S24 Ultra isn't just a device; it's a dynamic and ever-evolving companion that ensures users stay at the forefront of technology.

# CHAPTER 8

## ACCESSORIES AND ENHANCEMENTS

### Elevating the Experience with Galaxy S24 Accessories

The array of accessories designed to complement and enhance the device transforms it into a versatile and personalized companion. From protective cases to cutting-edge wearables, each accessory contributes to a seamless integration of technology into the user's lifestyle.

Protecting the Galaxy S24 Ultra is more than just a practical consideration; it's an opportunity to express personal style. A variety of protective cases, ranging from sleek and minimalist designs to rugged and robust options, cater to diverse preferences. These cases not only shield the device from daily wear and tear but also serve as a canvas for personal expression, allowing users to showcase their individuality.

Charging accessories play a pivotal role in ensuring that the Galaxy S24 Ultra stays powered up throughout the day. Wireless charging pads, optimized for the device, offer a cable-free and convenient charging solution. Fast-charging adapters and cables ensure that users can top up their device quickly, minimizing downtime and keeping them connected to what matters most.

The Galaxy S24 Ultra's compatibility with a range of wearables further expands its capabilities. Smartwatches, fitness trackers, and wireless earbuds seamlessly integrate with the device, creating a holistic ecosystem. The wearables are not just accessories; they enhance the user experience by providing real-time health and fitness data, quick access to notifications, and immersive audio experiences.

Samsung's commitment to innovation extends to its range of accessories, with advancements that redefine how users interact with their devices. Cutting-edge accessories like the S Pen stylus offer a new dimension of creativity and productivity. The S Pen transforms the Galaxy S24 Ultra into a digital canvas, allowing users to jot down notes, sketch, and navigate the device with precision.

Enhancing audio experiences is a key focus for Samsung's accessory lineup. High-quality wireless earbuds and headphones provide immersive sound, whether users are listening to music, watching videos, or taking calls. The seamless integration of audio accessories ensures that users can enjoy a premium audio experience that complements the device's multimedia capabilities.

Navigating through the Galaxy S24 accessories is a user-friendly experience, aligning with Samsung's commitment to accessibility. The SmartThings app serves as a central hub for managing and connecting compatible accessories. This centralized approach ensures that users can effortlessly customize their device's ecosystem, whether it's adjusting smart home settings or monitoring fitness goals.

Beyond functionality, Samsung's accessories are designed with a focus on aesthetics and comfort. From premium leather cases to ergonomic wearables, each accessory is crafted with attention to detail. The design philosophy reflects Samsung's commitment to providing users with not just functional additions but accessories that seamlessly blend with their lifestyle.

Customization is at the forefront of the accessory experience for the Galaxy S24 Ultra. Users can personalize their devices with a range of interchangeable bands, covers, and stylus options. This level of customization ensures that the accessories become an extension of the user's style, allowing them to curate a device ecosystem that reflects their personality.

The Samsung Galaxy S24 Ultra's array of accessories is not just an addition; it's an integral part of the user experience. From protective cases to cutting-edge wearables, each accessory is meticulously designed to elevate the device's functionality, style, and versatility. Samsung's commitment to innovation and user-centric design is evident in every accessory, contributing to a seamless and personalized integration of technology into the user's daily life.

## Tips for Maximizing Your Device's Potential

Unlocking the full potential of the Samsung Galaxy S24 Ultra involves more than just tapping into its impressive hardware and features; it's about leveraging smart tips and tricks to enhance your overall user experience. Whether you're a tech enthusiast or a casual user, these tips will help you make the most of your device's capabilities.

### 1. Customizing Your Home Screen

Tailor your home screen to suit your preferences. Long-press on the home screen to access options for widgets, wallpapers, and themes. Arrange your apps in a way that maximizes efficiency, creating a personalized layout that enhances navigation.

### 2. Gestures for Seamless Navigation

Explore gesture-based navigation for a fluid and intuitive experience. Swipe gestures can replace traditional navigation buttons, providing more screen real estate. Customize these gestures in the Settings menu under "Navigation."

### 3. Maximizing Battery Life

Optimize your device's battery life by managing background apps and adjusting settings. Explore the "Battery" section in Settings to enable power-saving modes, control background processes, and monitor battery usage. This ensures your device stays powered throughout the day.

### 4. Security Features

Leverage the security features of your Galaxy S24 Ultra. Set up biometric authentication, such as fingerprints or facial recognition, for secure and convenient device access. Explore the "Biometrics and Security" section in Settings for customization options.

### 5. Utilizing Split Screen and Multi-Window

Enhance multitasking by utilizing split-screen and multi-window features. Long-press the app overview button to activate split-screen mode, allowing you to run two apps simultaneously. This is particularly useful for productivity tasks or referencing information while browsing.

### 6. Smart Edge Panels

Make use of the Edge Panels feature for quick access to your favorite apps, contacts, and tools. Customize the Edge Panels in Settings to create shortcuts and improve accessibility. This feature provides a convenient way to navigate and multitask seamlessly.

### 7. Bixby Voice Commands

Explore Bixby, Samsung's virtual assistant, and make use of voice commands for hands-free interactions. Customize Bixby settings to suit your preferences, and discover how it can streamline tasks, provide information, and enhance your overall device usage.

### 8. Personalizing Quick Settings

Customize the Quick Settings menu to have quick access to the functions you use most frequently. Edit the order of icons, add or remove tiles, and tailor the menu to align with your preferences. This ensures you can efficiently toggle through essential settings.

### 9. Utilizing Wireless DeX

Experience a desktop-like environment by utilizing Wireless DeX. Connect your Galaxy S24 Ultra to a compatible TV or monitor wirelessly and transform your device into a desktop experience. Explore the "Connections" section in Settings to set up Wireless DeX.

### 10. Taking Advantage of Device Care

Regularly use the Device Care feature to optimize your device's performance. In the Settings menu, navigate to "Device care" to access tools for optimizing storage, managing battery usage, and keeping your device running smoothly.

### 11. Exploring Hidden Features

Dive deeper into your device by exploring hidden features. From hidden settings to lesser-known capabilities, there's often more to discover. Engage with online communities or forums to learn about tips and tricks shared by fellow users.

### 12. Regular Software Updates

Stay on top of software updates to ensure your device is equipped with the latest features, improvements, and security patches. Enable automatic updates in the Settings menu or regularly check for updates to keep your device running optimally.

# CHAPTER 9

## COMMON QUESTIONS AND TROUBLESHOOTING

### Frequently Asked Questions

Here are some frequently asked questions about the Samsung Galaxy S24 Ultra, along with detailed answers:

1. Q: What are the standout features of the Samsung Galaxy S24 Ultra?

A: The Galaxy S24 Ultra boasts a stunning large display, powerful camera system, advanced processor, and seamless integration with a range of accessories. It excels in performance, photography, and overall user experience.

2. Q: How is the camera system on the Galaxy S24 Ultra different from previous models?

A: The Galaxy S24 Ultra introduces a versatile rear camera setup with multiple lenses, catering to a wide range of photography styles. The advanced sensors and computational photography enhancements deliver exceptional image quality, especially in low-light conditions.

3. Q: Can the Galaxy S24 Ultra be wirelessly charged?

A: Yes, the Galaxy S24 Ultra supports wireless charging. This convenient feature allows users to charge their device without the need for cables, enhancing the overall charging experience.

4. Q: What accessories are compatible with the Galaxy S24 Ultra?

A: The Galaxy S24 Ultra is compatible with a variety of accessories, including protective cases, wireless chargers, wearables like smartwatches and fitness trackers, and the S Pen stylus for enhanced creativity and productivity.

5. Q: How does the device handle multitasking and split-screen functionalities?

A: The Galaxy S24 Ultra excels in multitasking with features like split-screen and multi-window. Users can run two apps simultaneously, enhancing productivity and providing a seamless experience for referencing information while using other apps.

6. Q: What security features does the Galaxy S24 Ultra offer?

A: The device provides advanced security features, including biometric authentication such as fingerprints and facial recognition. Users can customize security settings in the "Biometrics and Security" section to ensure secure and convenient access.

7. Q: How frequently does the Galaxy S24 Ultra receive software updates?

A: Samsung is committed to regularly updating the Galaxy S24 Ultra's software to ensure optimal performance, security, and access to the latest features. Users can enable automatic updates or manually check for updates in the Settings menu.

8. Q: Is the Galaxy S24 Ultra compatible with Wireless DeX?

A: Yes, the Galaxy S24 Ultra supports Wireless DeX, allowing users to wirelessly connect their device to a compatible TV or monitor and experience a desktop-like environment. This feature provides versatility for work and entertainment.

9. Q: What are some tips for maximizing battery life on the Galaxy S24 Ultra?

A: Users can optimize battery life by managing background apps, adjusting settings in the "Battery" section, and exploring power-saving modes. These tips help ensure that the device stays powered throughout the day.

10. Q: Can I use Bixby voice commands on the Galaxy S24 Ultra?

A: Yes, Bixby, Samsung's virtual assistant, is available on the Galaxy S24 Ultra. Users can utilize voice commands for hands-free interactions, streamlining tasks and accessing information with voice control.

11. Q: How can I customize the home screen and gestures on the Galaxy S24 Ultra?

A: Users can customize the home screen by long-pressing to access options for widgets, wallpapers, and themes. Gesture-based navigation can be configured in the Settings menu under "Navigation" for a personalized and intuitive experience.

12. Q: Are there hidden features on the Galaxy S24 Ultra?
A: Yes, the device often includes hidden features beyond the standard settings. Exploring online communities or forums can help users discover lesser-known capabilities and tips for maximizing their device's potential.

## Troubleshooting Common Issues

Addressing common issues is crucial for maintaining a seamless experience with the Samsung Galaxy S24 Ultra. Here's a troubleshooting guide to help users navigate and resolve potential challenges:

1. Battery Draining Quickly
Possible Solution: Check for apps running in the background and close unnecessary ones. Adjust screen

brightness, and explore battery settings to identify power-hungry apps. Consider enabling power-saving modes for extended battery life.

2. Device Overheating

Possible Solution: Overheating may occur during intensive tasks. Close unused apps, limit simultaneous processes, and avoid prolonged usage in direct sunlight. If the issue persists, check for software updates, as they may include optimizations.

3. Connectivity Issues (Wi-Fi or Mobile Data)

Possible Solution: Restart the device, toggle airplane mode on and off, and ensure Wi-Fi/mobile data is enabled. If the issue persists, check for network-related outages, update network settings, or reset network connections in the device settings.

4. Slow Performance or Lag

Possible Solution: Close background apps, clear cached data, and restart the device to free up system resources. If the problem persists, check for software updates, and consider disabling unnecessary animations in the device settings.

5. App Crashes or Freezes:
Possible Solution: Update the problematic app, clear app cache, or reinstall the app. If the issue persists, check for device software updates, as they may include fixes for app-related bugs.

6. Camera Not Functioning Properly
Possible Solution: Restart the device, check for software updates, and ensure there's enough storage space for photos. If the problem persists, clear the camera app cache or try using a third-party camera app to identify if the issue is app-specific.

7. Device Not Charging
Possible Solution: Verify that you are using a compatible charging cable and adapter. Clean the charging port from dust or debris, and try a different power source. If the issue persists, test with another charger to identify whether the problem lies with the charging accessories.

8. Touchscreen Responsiveness Issues
Possible Solution: Clean the screen, remove screen protectors if applicable, and restart the device. If the

problem persists, check for software updates, as they may include improvements to touchscreen responsiveness.

## 9. Bluetooth Connectivity Problems

Possible Solution: Ensure Bluetooth is enabled, restart the device, and check for software updates. If the issue persists, forget and re-pair the Bluetooth device, and ensure it is within the recommended range for connectivity.

## 10. Storage Running Low

Possible Solution: Review and clear unnecessary files, apps, or media to free up storage space. Consider transferring media files to an external storage device or cloud service. Regularly check and manage storage in the device settings.

## 11. Device Not Responding or Frozen

Possible Solution: Perform a soft reset by holding down the power and volume down buttons simultaneously. If the problem persists, consider a factory reset after backing up essential data. This helps to resolve software-related issues.

12. Security or Authentication Issues

Possible Solution: Update security settings, reconfigure biometric authentication, and check for software updates that may include security patches. If

# CONCLUSION

I want to express my heartfelt gratitude for choosing this book as your guide to exploring the remarkable features and capabilities of the Samsung Galaxy S24 Ultra. Your decision to embark on this technological exploration is sincerely appreciated, and I hope that the information provided has enriched your understanding of this cutting-edge device.

In the ever-evolving landscape of technology, staying informed is key, and your commitment to learning about the Galaxy S24 Ultra reflects your passion for innovation. This book aimed to go beyond the specifications and features, delving into the practical aspects and user experiences that make this device a standout in the smartphone market.

First and foremost, I want to express my sincere appreciation for your time and attention. I understand that your time is valuable, and I aimed to provide you with content that is insightful, informative, and engaging. Exploring the features, functionalities, and tips for maximizing the potential of the Galaxy S24 Ultra has been a shared journey, and I am grateful to have had the opportunity to be your guide.

As a token of my gratitude, I would like to take a moment to thank you for choosing this book. In the vast world of information, your decision to trust me as a source of knowledge is something I do not take lightly. I hope that the content has lived up to your expectations and provided you with valuable insights into the device that is reshaping the way we interact with technology.

"The Samsung Galaxy S24 Ultra: Unveiling Innovation" was crafted with the intention of serving as a comprehensive resource for both tech enthusiasts and casual users alike. From detailed descriptions of the device's features to practical tips for enhancing your user experience, I endeavored to cover a spectrum of topics that cater to various interests and needs.

I acknowledge that the world of technology is dynamic, and updates and innovations continue to shape the landscape. I encourage you to stay curious, explore new features and updates as they become available, and continue to make the most of your Samsung Galaxy S24

Ultra. This device is not just a tool; it's a companion in your daily life, and I hope that the knowledge gained from this book enhances your interactions with it.

As we bid farewell to these pages, I want to leave you with a sense of empowerment. The Galaxy S24 Ultra is more than just a smartphone; it's a gateway to a world of possibilities. Whether you're capturing breathtaking moments with its advanced camera system, optimizing your productivity with its performance capabilities, or personalizing your experience with its array of accessories, this device is designed to adapt to your lifestyle.

Once again, thank you for choosing "The Samsung Galaxy S24 Ultra: Unveiling Innovation." Your support means the world to me, and I sincerely hope that this book has been a valuable companion on your journey of discovery. If you ever find yourself with new questions or in need of updated information, know that the world of technology is vast, and there's always more to explore.

Wishing you endless joy and productivity with your Samsung Galaxy S24 Ultra. May it continue to be a source of inspiration, connection, and convenience in your daily life.

www.ingramcontent.com/pod-product-compliance
Lightning Source LLC
Chambersburg PA
CBHW071305050326
40690CB00011B/2533